NATIONAL GEOGRAPHIC

D0584318

Ladders

Symbols
of
Liberty
AMERICAN WONDERS

THE National Mall

by Sheri Reda
illustrated by Eric Larsen

The National Mall in Washington, D.C., isn't some sort of patriotic shopping center. It's a long, green lawn lined with trees and museums, and it's a great spot for parades and political events. It's also the go-to place for checking out the most famous American **monuments**, structures that honor important people and events. These monuments are powerful **symbols** of liberty. They represent liberty and other ideals Americans have fought for throughout our nation's history.

Washington Monument

The Lincoln Memorial, completed in 1922, has 36 marble columns. There is one column for each of the states in the Union when Lincoln died in 1865.

Lincoln Memorial Reflecting Pool

Martin Luther King, Jr. Memorial

Lincoln Memorial

The Reflecting Pool between the Lincoln Memorial and the Washington Monument is more than 2,000 feet long but only up to 30 inches deep.

The Martin Luther King, Jr. Memorial, cut from solid stone, is the Mall's newest monument and a tribute to a national hero.

The National Mall extends from the U.S. Capitol to the Lincoln Memorial almost two miles away. The Capitol is where Congress meets to make our laws.

U.S. Capitol

Capitol Reflecting Pool

The Capitol Reflecting Pool was added to the Mall in the 1970s. It reflects the U.S. Capitol and attracts many visitors.

Mall lawn

Completed in 1884, the Washington Monument is the oldest and tallest monument on the Mall.

The Jefferson Memorial was completed in 1943. It overlooks the Tidal Basin, a body of water connected to the nearby Potomac River.

Jefferson Memorial

cherry trees

In 1912, Japan sent the United States a gift of more than 3,000 cherry trees, which were planted on the Mall. Many people visit the Mall in the spring when these trees are in bloom.

Check In Who are some of the famous Americans honored here? Which monument would you visit first, and why?

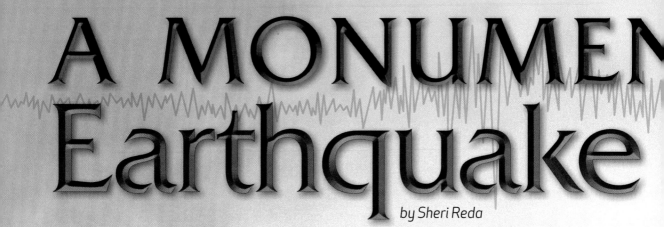

A MONUMEN
Earthquake

by Sheri Reda

Look up while you're standing next to the Washington Monument, and you might wonder if the pyramid-shaped top of the structure pierces the sky. Tourists can't miss the nearly 555-foot monument that towers over the National Mall to honor our first president.

The Washington Monument is a fitting tribute to a man who proved he was a great leader. George Washington was appointed the head of the American army shortly after fighting broke out between the colonies and Great Britain in 1775. This was the beginning of the American Revolution. Later, Washington was elected president of the newly formed nation. He served two terms as the country's leader.

On any typical afternoon, hundreds of tourists can be found roaming the Washington Monument's grounds.

Visitors who climb the tower's 897 steps or take the elevator to the top are rewarded with breathtaking views of the Mall, the White House, Washington, D.C.—even the states of Maryland and Virginia in the distance. However, on the afternoon of August 23, 2011, tourists felt the tower begin to rattle and shake. Small pieces of stone fell from the ceiling. Startled tourists glanced up in confusion. Was it the wind? An accident?

It was an **earthquake**, a violent movement in Earth's crust. The quake shook the entire East Coast, including Washington, D.C.

> Inspectors check for damage to the Washington Monument after the earthquake.

CRITAL

Washington, D.C.

Mineral, Virginia ●

The source of the earthquake was near the town of Mineral, Virginia. That's more than 80 miles southwest of Washington, D.C. People as far away as New York, Georgia, and Illinois reported feeling the quake.

The Damage Done

The national park rangers who serve as tour guides for the monument quickly began to evacuate tourists from the structure, guiding them out of the building and away from danger. The rangers' efforts were successful. Several people were "shaken" by the quake, but no one was hurt.

After the ground stopped shaking and the dust settled, it was time to inspect the monument for damage. Experts started at the top of the monument and **rappelled** (ruh-PEHLD) down the outside of the tower to examine each of its stone blocks. Several of the blocks were damaged. Six blocks at the top had cracks running through the entire thick piece of stone. The **mortar** between the blocks was broken in many places. Based on the amount of damage they found, the inspectors declared the building unsafe and closed it to the public until repairs could be made.

> Workers balance on metal scaffolding as they repair and strengthen the monument after it was damaged by the earthquake.

The earthquake that rocked the Washington Monument was strong enough to crack the building and break off this chunk of marble.

FACTS ABOUT THE WASHINGTON MONUMENT

- The Washington Monument's 36,491 stone blocks weigh just a bit more than 81,000 tons. That doesn't include the 20,000-ton foundation.

- The monument is a traditional Egyptian **obelisk** (AH-buh-lisk), a tall, four-sided tower with a pyramid at the top.

- The monument is the tallest freestanding stone building in the world.

- The walls are 15 feet thick at the base but only 18 inches thick near the top, where the monument narrows.

- Not everyone liked the final design for the Washington Monument. Architect Robert Mills had developed a different, more complicated design. He complained that the monument would look like an asparagus stalk.

Built to Last

The damage to the Washington Monument could have been worse if the construction crews who built it hadn't taken their time to carefully put up the tower of white granite stone. In fact, it took more than 40 years to build it! Construction on the Washington Monument began in 1848, but just a few years into the project, work stopped due to a lack of funds. Then, with only one-third of the monument complete, the Civil War began. That delayed construction even further. At 156 feet tall, the unfinished monument looked more like a chimney than a grand tower. Finally, in 1888, the tower was completed and open to visitors. People flocked to Washington, D.C., to see it. They marveled at the massive stone tower. It was the tallest building in the world at that time. And it had been built to last, even during an earthquake.

Today, the Washington Monument still stands as a symbol of our nation and a monument to our nation's first president, but significant repairs and new safety features are needed to make sure it remains safe if another earthquake occurs. The building will reopen for tours once it is completely updated and repaired. In the meantime, the most recognizable monument on the Mall is still a beautiful site for patriotic celebrations.

The Washington Monument still had its scaffolding in place on July 4, 2013. Even so, it was a perfect place to watch the fireworks.

Check In What parts of the Washington Monument received the most damage from the earthquake?

The Making of a Memorial

by Hugh Westrup

A champion of liberty. That's how Americans view Thomas Jefferson, one of our nation's founders and the third president of the United States. Jefferson was the main author of the Declaration of Independence, the document that told the British that the American colonies would fight for their freedom. His essays and speeches have taught us the importance of independence. It's easy to see why, in 1934, when Franklin D. Roosevelt was our 32nd president, the U.S. Congress approved the creation of a memorial to Jefferson in Washington, D.C. But creating the monument was easier said

than done. Where would the monument be located? What would it look like? These questions and more had to be answered before construction could begin. Congress appointed a group of people to make all of these decisions.

The site they selected had a perfect view of the White House, which was important, but it was right in the middle of a grove of cherry trees. This posed a problem: the trees would have to be moved in order to build the monument. The city of Tokyo, Japan, had presented the beautiful trees to Washington, D.C., as a gift. Many were concerned that moving them might offend the Japanese. Uprooting the trees also could damage them. No one wanted the cherry trees to be harmed—even if the monument site did have a "perfect view." In the end, builders did move some of the cherry trees to new locations to fit the memorial into this ideal spot. Many cherry trees still surround the monument.

Protesters chained themselves to cherry trees in 1938 to try to prevent them from being moved to make way for the memorial.

An Ancient Design

With the location settled, it was time to determine the design of the monument. The Jefferson Memorial's designers, including **architect** John Russell Pope, wanted it to look like the ancient Roman Pantheon, built 1,800 years earlier in Rome, Italy. The design of the Pantheon features **columns** in the front and a **dome** for a roof. Throughout his career as an architect, Pope had designed other buildings based on the styles of ancient Greece and Rome.

The Pantheon is a temple to the Roman gods. Until modern times, it had the largest dome (shown at the top) ever built.

The architect drew plans for the inside and outside of the memorial. These plans are called blueprints, and they show how to construct the building.

Jefferson designed this building at the University of Virginia. He got his inspiration from the Pantheon.

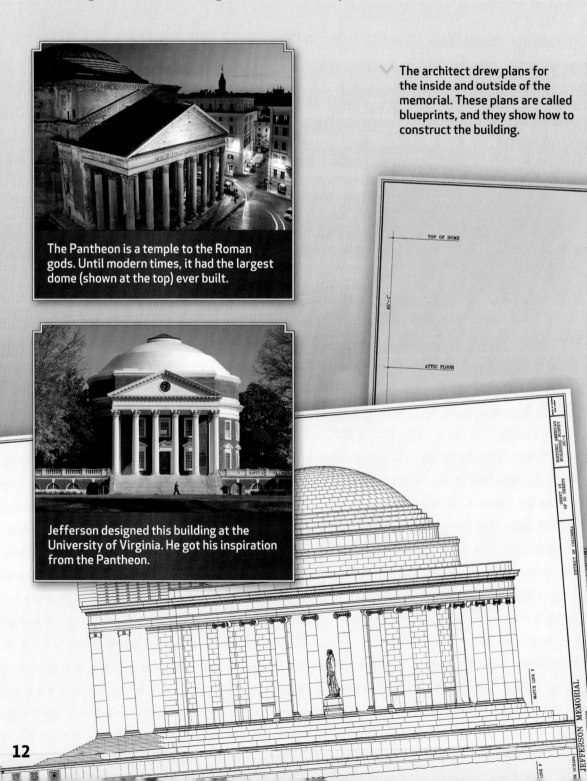

Pope and the designers had a good reason to pick this ancient design. Jefferson, an architect himself, had modeled several buildings he designed on the Pantheon. However, not everyone liked this ancient Roman look. Some argued that a memorial built in the 20th century should look modern, not ancient. They called the planned structure a "misfit" and an "insult to the memory of Thomas Jefferson." But President Franklin D. Roosevelt liked the ancient design. He ended the argument and allowed the builders to move ahead with the design for the Jefferson Memorial.

The Chrysler Building in New York City was built only a few years before the Jefferson Memorial. Its sleek look shows the modern style of architecture that some would have preferred for the memorial.

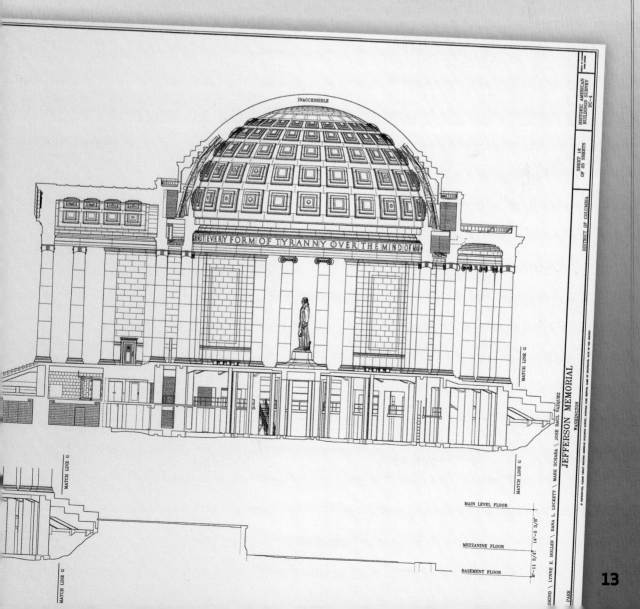

Powerful Words, Powerful Statue

Thomas Jefferson was a famous writer and speaker, and his words carried great power. It made sense to incorporate Jefferson's most influential words into his memorial. But which quotations best represented Jefferson's beliefs? One quotation the committee chose came from the second line of the Declaration of Independence:

> "We hold these truths to be self-evident: that all men are created equal, that they are endowed by their Creator with certain inalienable rights, among these are life, liberty and the pursuit of happiness . . ."

Those famous words are part of a quotation carved on a stone panel on the inside wall of the memorial. Some people complained about the quotation because Jefferson wasn't the only writer of the document. They argued that these words might not really be his.

Four other memorable quotations appear on the inside wall of the monument. These quotations had to be edited—words had to be taken out—so they would fit on the panels and be easier to read. Some people felt the edited quotations were not really what Jefferson said or wrote.

The design for the memorial called for a tall, impressive bronze statue of Thomas Jefferson at its center. At least that was the plan. But the United States was fighting in a war in 1943 when the memorial opened. The nation needed metal for the war, to build tanks, airplanes, warships, and weapons. So the builders could not use bronze for the statue. Instead, they had to build a plaster statue coated in bronze paint. Only when the war was over could they replace the plaster statue with a magnificent bronze one that truly honors this great leader.

The National Park Service reports that more than two million people visit the Jefferson Memorial each year.

WE HOLD THESE TRUTHS TO BE SELF-EVIDENT: THAT ALL MEN ARE CREATED EQUAL. THAT THEY ARE ENDOWED BY THEIR CREATOR WITH CERTAIN INALIENABLE RIGHTS. AMONG THESE ARE LIFE, LIBERTY AND THE PURSUIT OF HAPPINESS. THAT TO SECURE THESE RIGHTS GOVERNMENTS ARE INSTITUTED AMONG MEN. WE··· SOLEMNLY PUBLISH AND DECLARE, THAT THESE COLONIES ARE AND OF RIGHT OUGHT TO BE FREE AND INDEPENDENT STATES···AND FOR THE SUPPORT OF THIS DECLARATION, WITH A FIRM RELIANCE ON THE PROTECTION OF DIVINE PROVIDENCE, WE MUTUALLY PLEDGE OUR LIVES, OUR FORTUNES AND OUR SACRED HONOUR.

Check In   How does this memorial honor Jefferson's words and deeds?

15

HONORING HONEST ABE

by Elizabeth Massie
illustrated by David Harrington

Some people are "larger than life." Abraham Lincoln was one of those people. Through hard work and determination, Lincoln grew from a country boy to a successful lawyer and finally to the 16th president of the United States. The challenges and experiences he faced growing up helped shape the president he would become.

ABE LINCOLN WAS BORN IN KENTUCKY ON FEBRUARY 12, 1809. HIS FAMILY MOVED TO THE INDIANA FRONTIER IN 1816. A FRONTIER IS AN AREA SETTLED BY PEOPLE NEXT TO A WILDERNESS. THERE, THE FAMILY BUILT A CABIN AND STRUGGLED TO SURVIVE, RAISING VEGETABLES AND ANIMALS FOR FOOD.

WHAT A STRONG, HARDWORKING BOY! I IMAGINE HE'LL DO GREAT THINGS WHEN HE GROWS UP.

THOUGH HE RARELY ATTENDED SCHOOL, ABE LOVED TO READ, AND HE ALMOST ALWAYS CARRIED A BORROWED BOOK WITH HIM. HIS DESIRE TO LEARN HELPED PREPARE HIM FOR HIS LIFE'S CHALLENGES.

THE THINGS I WANT TO KNOW ARE IN BOOKS. MY BEST FRIEND IS THE MAN WHO'LL GET ME A BOOK I HAVEN'T READ.

ABE DID ODD JOBS FOR NEIGHBORING FARMERS TO MAKE EXTRA MONEY TO HELP HIS FAMILY. ONE JOB WAS SPLITTING WOOD INTO RAILS FOR FENCES. HE WAS SO GOOD AT IT THAT HE GOT THE NICKNAME "RAIL SPLITTER." LEARNING THE VALUE OF HARD WORK ALSO HELPED PREPARE HIM FOR THE FUTURE.

WHEN ABE WAS 19, HE BUILT A FLATBOAT. A FLATBOAT IS PRETTY MUCH WHAT IT SOUNDS LIKE—A BOAT WITH A FLAT BOTTOM MADE TO CARRY GOODS ALONG A WATERWAY. IN 1828, ABE AND ANOTHER MAN LOADED A FLATBOAT WITH GOODS AND SAILED SOUTH ON THE MISSISSIPPI RIVER TO NEW ORLEANS.

HEAR THAT ROAR? THERE'S ROUGH WATER AHEAD!

PULL HARD, ABE! WE'LL KEEP THIS BOAT AFLOAT!

IT WAS IN NEW ORLEANS THAT ABE SAW A SLAVE MARKET, WHERE SLAVE TRADERS BOUGHT AND SOLD ENSLAVED PEOPLE TO WORK ON PLANTATIONS. A PLANTATION IS A VERY LARGE FARM. ABE WAS ANGRY AND UPSET TO SEE THESE PEOPLE TREATED SO HORRIBLY—BEATEN, CHAINED, AND FORCED TO OBEY THEIR "MASTERS." THIS EXPERIENCE SHAPED ABE'S OPINIONS ABOUT SLAVERY.

THEY'RE SELLING THAT WOMAN TO ONE PLANTATION OWNER AND HER TINY CHILD TO ANOTHER! HOW CAN THIS HAPPEN IN A LAND OF FREEDOM?

WHEN ABE WAS A YOUNG MAN, HE WORKED IN A STORE. ONE DAY HE REALIZED HE'D CHARGED A WOMAN A FEW TOO MANY PENNIES FOR SOMETHING SHE'D BOUGHT. HE DIDN'T HESITATE TO WALK SEVERAL MILES TO THE WOMAN'S HOME TO GIVE THE WOMAN HER PENNIES BACK.

I'M SORRY, MA'AM. I ACCIDENTALLY CHARGED YOU TOO MUCH.

WHY, THANK YOU, ABE. I WISH ALL MERCHANTS WERE AS HONEST AS YOU!

MY RICH NEIGHBOR CLAIMS THAT PART OF MY LAND IS HIS. I DON'T KNOW WHAT TO DO!

IT ISN'T RIGHT THAT YOU'RE HAVING THIS MUCH TROUBLE! LET ME TALK TO THE TOWN COUNCIL ABOUT THIS.

WORKING IN THE STORE GAVE ABE THE CHANCE TO TALK TO HIS NEIGHBORS AND GET TO KNOW THEIR CONCERNS. HEARING PEOPLE'S CONCERNS AND WANTING TO HELP LED ABE TO AN INTEREST IN POLITICS AND LAW.

19

ABE'S INTEREST IN THE LAW GREW, SO HE DECIDED TO STUDY TO BECOME A LAWYER. HE WORKED AT HIS JOB DURING THE DAY AND STUDIED LAW ON HIS OWN AT NIGHT WITH BORROWED BOOKS. HE TRAVELED LONG DISTANCES TO WATCH LAWYERS WORK IN COURT. ABE PUT AS MUCH EFFORT INTO HIS LAW STUDIES AS HE HAD PUT INTO SPLITTING RAILS.

THERE'S NO WAY I CAN AFFORD LAW SCHOOL. IT'S A GOOD THING JUDGE DRUMMOND LETS ME BORROW HIS BOOKS.

AS A LAWYER, ABE WORKED TO FIND COMMON GROUND BETWEEN PEOPLE WHO HAD DISAGREEMENTS. IN FACT, HE SAW THE MAIN ROLE OF A LAWYER AS BEING A PEACEMAKER. THIS VIEW WOULD BE VERY IMPORTANT TO HIM WHEN HE BECAME A POLITICAL LEADER.

CALM DOWN, GENTLEMEN. I'M SURE WE CAN FIND A WORKABLE COMPROMISE.

A HOUSE DIVIDED AGAINST ITSELF CANNOT STAND!

BY 1858, ABE WAS SPEAKING OUT AGAINST SLAVERY IN THE TERRITORIES. A TERRITORY WAS A PART OF THE NATION THAT WAS NOT YET A STATE. IN THE FAMOUS DEBATES OF 1858 BETWEEN LINCOLN AND THE POLITICIAN, STEPHEN DOUGLAS, LINCOLN ARGUED THAT THE NATION COULD NOT SURVIVE IF HALF OF THE STATES CONDEMNED SLAVERY AND HALF OF THE STATES SUPPORTED SLAVERY.

TO THE SURPRISE OF MANY, LINCOLN WAS ELECTED PRESIDENT IN 1860. THE DISAGREEMENTS OVER SLAVERY BETWEEN THE NORTHERN STATES—THE NORTH—AND THE SOUTHERN STATES—THE SOUTH—WERE GROWING WORSE. HE REALIZED HE HAD TO BRING TOGETHER PEOPLE WHO DISAGREED IN ORDER TO SOLVE THESE SERIOUS PROBLEMS.

ABRAHAM LINCOLN WAS ELECTED PRESIDENT FOR A SECOND TIME IN 1864. IN MARCH OF 1865, HE SAID HIS GOAL FOR THE NATION WAS "LASTING PEACE AMONG OURSELVES." THE CIVIL WAR ENDED ONE MONTH LATER. THEN, ON APRIL 14, 1865, ABRAHAM LINCOLN WAS SHOT AND KILLED BY A SUPPORTER OF THE SOUTH, JOHN WILKES BOOTH. THE NATION MOURNED THEIR BELOVED PRESIDENT.

THE LINCOLN MEMORIAL IN WASHINGTON, D.C., OPENED IN 1922 TO HONOR LINCOLN. IT IS A STATELY, IMPRESSIVE BUILDING WITH COLUMNS AND 98 STEPS LEADING UP FROM THE REFLECTING POOL IN FRONT OF IT. THE STATUE OF LINCOLN INSIDE THE MONUMENT IS 19 FEET TALL. THE WORDS CARVED ABOVE THE STATUE SAY IT ALL: "IN THIS TEMPLE, AS IN THE HEARTS OF THE PEOPLE FOR WHOM HE SAVED THE UNION, THE MEMORY OF ABRAHAM LINCOLN IS ENSHRINED [HONORED] FOREVER."

HE WAS A REMARKABLE MAN.

IF I WORK HARDER NOW, MAYBE I CAN GROW UP TO BE A GREAT LEADER LIKE HONEST ABE.

HE'S MY FAVORITE PRESIDENT!

Check In How did Lincoln's early life experiences shape him into a leader of our country?

The Story of a Dream

by Becky Manfredini

He had a dream—a dream that people of all races could work together for freedom and equality. Dr. Martin Luther King, Jr. dreamed that all U.S. citizens would have equal rights, no matter what the color of their skin was or how rich or poor they were. He led the struggle for **civil rights** to make his dream come true.

Dr. King faced threats, violence, and jail time from those who disagreed with him. But he never gave up his fight. He always used peaceful methods. This process was slow, but it was steady and effective.

Dr. Martin Luther King, Jr. attends a meeting of a civil rights group he started in the 1950s.

The story of Dr. King's dream began on January 15, 1929, when he was born in Atlanta, Georgia. His parents, Reverend Martin Luther King, Sr. and Alberta Williams King, provided a happy family life for young Martin and his brother and sister.

Young Martin got his first taste of **segregation** at the age of six. Two white friends told him that their parents wouldn't let them play with him. At that time, laws in the southern part of the United States separated black and white citizens in many parts of public life. For example, black and white children could not eat at the same restaurants, drink from the same water fountains, or attend the same schools.

Martin was a bright student. He was accepted to Morehouse College, an all-black school, at the age of 15. But Martin wanted to follow in his father's footsteps and pursue a career in the church. He became a minister before finishing college.

Marching to Freedom

As a minister, Dr. King was determined to fight discrimination, or unfair treatment of people. He preached the message of equality in his church, and he began leading peaceful protests throughout the South to ensure that black and white citizens received the same rights.

In 1955, another courageous person joined Dr. King's quest to fight segregation. In Montgomery, Alabama, a bus driver told Rosa Parks, a black woman, to give up her seat to a white man. Parks refused to give up her seat, and she was put in jail. Dr. King supported Parks's action and led a yearlong bus **boycott**. African Americans refused to ride the buses at all in Montgomery. The boycott was a success because it took away from the profits of the bus company. In 1956, the U.S. Supreme Court ordered the city to allow blacks and whites to sit together on buses.

But buses, schools, and stores weren't the only places where civil rights were disregarded. In 1870, the 15th Amendment to the U.S. Constitution

Dr. King changed our nation by leading peaceful marches. Here, Dr. King and his wife Coretta take part in the March Against Fear in 1966. They walked more than 200 miles from Memphis, Tennessee, to Jackson, Mississippi.

gave black men the right to vote. Yet unfair laws still lingered. They made it difficult and sometimes even impossible for some African Americans to vote. Some people had to pass a reading and writing test before they could register to vote. Poor people were told they had to pay a tax to vote. In 1957, Dr. King inspired thousands of people to stand up for equal voting rights during a demonstration in Washington, D.C.

By 1960, both black and white citizens were working hard to promote civil rights. Dr. King encouraged black college students to conduct peaceful "sit-ins." They sat in whites-only areas in restaurants and refused to leave until they were served. Many restaurants called the police. The police arrested the protesters. These protests made the national news, and people around the country began to understand the injustice the African Americans faced.

In many places in the South, black and white citizens could not use the same restrooms or waiting areas.

Dr. Martin Luther King, Jr. married Coretta Scott in 1953. The couple lived in Montgomery, Alabama. They had four children, Yolanda, Martin, Dexter, and Bernice.

The Dream Grows

In August of 1963, Dr. King led 250,000 people in the March on Washington for Jobs and Freedom. Thousand of Americans of all races gathered on the National Mall to hear civil rights leaders speak and singers perform in support of the movement. But they all were waiting for Dr. King to take the podium in front of the Lincoln Memorial.

He stood before the statue of Lincoln, a man whose efforts and vision helped free the nation from the chains of slavery. Dr. King's powerful voice

The peaceful March on Washington was broadcast to a national television audience. It brought many Americans face-to-face with the Civil Rights Movement.

rose as a hush fell on crowd. He had prepared a short speech, but soon, Dr. King began to speak from the heart.

Afterwards, Dr. King told graduate student Donald Smith, "*I started out reading the speech . . . the audience response was wonderful that day. . . . And all of a sudden this thing came to me . . . 'I have a dream . . .'*" At that moment, he stopped reading the speech he had prepared. Instead, he talked passionately about his dream for freedom and equality. This now-famous address is known as his "I Have a Dream" speech. His stirring words inspired millions to understand and take up the cause of civil rights and justice.

"I Have a Dream" remains one of the most heartfelt and stirring speeches in support of civil rights.

Remember the Dream

At the age of 35, Dr. King became the youngest person awarded the Nobel Peace Prize, an honor given to people who promote peace worldwide. He donated the award money to fund the Civil Rights Movement and continued pursuing his dream. On April 4, 1968, however, Dr. King was shot and killed in Memphis, Tennessee. The nation was shocked by the news and mourned a great loss. But Dr. King continues to inspire people of all ages and races to fight against discrimination throughout the world.

Today, his dream lives on at the Martin Luther King, Jr. National Memorial in Washington, D.C. It is located near the Lincoln Memorial, where he gave his

Dr. King's image is carved in a rock called the "Stone of Hope."

"I Have a Dream" speech. Dr. King's monument features his image carved in stone. It looks as if Dr. King is emerging from a piece of rough, solid rock. The image of this great leader stands determined and dignified, as always, against the backdrop of a clear, blue sky.

Dr. King's **legacy** continues to this day. Americans feel it strongly, especially in January on Martin Luther King, Jr. Day. That's a national holiday that honors his life and work. Dr. King's tireless efforts to fight discrimination led to the Civil Rights Act of 1964. This law forbids discrimination based on race or gender. His determination paved the way for Congress to pass the Voting Rights Act of 1965, which removed the unfair practices that had kept African Americans from being able to vote. Today, we are closer than ever to ensuring all Americans enjoy the same civil rights, thanks to the efforts of Dr. Martin Luther King, Jr. and those who followed and supported him.

> *"If you can't fly then run, if you can't run then walk, if you can't walk then crawl, but whatever you do you have to keep moving forward."* —DR. MARTIN LUTHER KING, JR.

Check In How did Dr. Martin Luther King, Jr. use peaceful measures to fight for civil rights?

31

Discuss

1. What connections can you make among the five selections in this book? How are the selections related?

2. What is a symbol of liberty? How are the monuments on the National Mall symbols of liberty? Can you think of any others?

3. What were some of Abraham Lincoln's personal qualities that made him a great leader?

4. Dr. Martin Luther King, Jr. dreamed of equality and justice for all Americans. In your opinion, has this dream come true? Explain your answer.

5. What else do you want to know about the famous leaders from our past who inspired these monuments? How can you find out more?